Moll Anderson

EXTRA SPECIAL Thanks

To my son Michael, who has become an incredible person, wonderful businessman, and a fabulous husband to his beautiful wife, Aphrodite. I am so proud of you both! To Hayley and her husband, Aaron, and to Chase and Lauren—you are all so uniquely blessed and live in excellence. I am proud to be your stepmom.

To my mother, Mary Ellen "Kay" Ruffalo, who is the ultimate diva and is always a "Glamorous Hostess" to this day, even at the age of 83. To William Taft Ruffalo—Dad, I will miss you forever, and you're still the most dapper man I ever knew. To my mother- and father-in-law, Hilda and Charles Anderson, thank you for your love and for raising the most amazing son and husband. To my family— the Keaggys and the Ruffalos and the Andersons. To Karen (my best bud) and John Hall for their undying friendship and talented contributions to this book. To Kitty Moon Emery for believing in me and, most important, for introducing me to my husband, Charlie. To Stacie Standifer—it's an honor to have my column in *Nashville Lifestyles* magazine! To Bobbie McCloud and Deb Staver—I miss working with you both and I will always be an honorary Patton. To Susan Anderson for being such a great sister. To Penny, who is my sister-friend and my angel's mother. To Dee Haslam for always giving so much support in friendship and with Rivr Media. To all my fabulous clients who blessed me with a hugely successful business—you know who you are.

To "Team Moll": Linda Willey, my dear friend and executive director of our foundation, and Ashley Cate, who is amazingly creative and talented and truly like a daughter. I cannot function without Pat Adair, who is our Pat-O! To Elder Carrillo; Marilyn Spears, aka Sophie's other mom; and Britta Bollinger, you are the ultimate flower child. Our star, Ashlyne Huff. To Brady Wardlaw, who is fabulously talented with my hair and makeup. To Karen Hosack for all you do. To Cindy Games, who has been along for the ride from the first book and who is now vice president, publisher of Moll Anderson Productions. To my agents Deb Goldfarb and Puraj Puri—I'm so happy to be home again at Rebel.

To my girlfriends Missy, Jinger, Sherri, Barbara, Catherine, Lori, Diane, Nancy, Pat, Marie, Loretta, Kathy, and Susan.

To Ken Downing and Bill Mackin from Neiman Marcus, and to B.J. Johnson and Steven Schellhaas from the Neiman Marcus Scottsdale, Arizona, store. To Agata Wisniewska and David Gray at Donna Karan. To Scott Meltzer at Michael Kors, and to Carolyn Mahboubi and Patrick Vos at Gucci. The support I have received and my new relationships enabled this book to be the real deal!

THE *Seductive* HOME™

MOLL ANDERSON

Dedication

I dedicate this book to the man who inspired me. He changed my life in the most wonderful way possible by being positive, full of love, and enjoying the little things that make a difference, like a cup of coffee together in the morning, flowers, music, or maybe a glass of wine together at the end of the day. Charlie, you made it possible for me to let go and finally be able to feel and experience everything I had always hoped for and believed possible in a relationship.

That's how The Seductive Home *was truly created, out of all the love and passion we infused into our home and life together. It was so much fun and so inspiring to me that it made me want to share the journey that I had only dreamed about. It's a choice to live in the moment and to truly stop, experience, and appreciate a relationship. You can create the life you have always dreamed of living!*

Thank you, Charlie, for believing the dream!

Love,

Seduction evokes emotion—it's exhilarating, joyful, surprising, and most important, it's sensual. You're drawn in and you want to experience more.

That defines what I call the "seductive home." It's always found in all the decadent details. The finishes, the textures on the walls, and how the paint color catches the light in such a way that you yourself are lit beautifully. It makes you feel flirty and fabulous.

When you walk into a seductive home, whether it's a one-room apartment or a mansion, everywhere you look you will feel excitement and you will be absolutely dazzled. Thoughts will start racing in your head and the next thing you know, they'll slip out as you say, "This room is so sexy," or "It's so old Hollywood," or "I'd like to curl up with a good book and a glass of wine." So, what defines the seductive home?

The fabrics are exquisite and voluptuous, from flowing drapes that define a room to the furniture that caresses you as you sit. And oh, you'll find yourself dreaming about waking up and rolling around for hours in the lush bed linens.

The fresh-cut flowers are always breathtaking. Whether it's one simple, delicate orchid, Cabernet-colored peonies, or a labyrinth of white Casablanca lilies cascading from a vase, flowers are alive and so vibrant in color that they have a powerful presence. They also add a sumptuous scent to any room.

Could I recreate this seductive lifestyle and actually feel like this all of the time?

Candles are burning everywhere. Their flickering light illuminates a space as well as fills the air with delectable sensory wilds that speak to your senses. Their aroma is unforgettable as it lingers softly, always the perfect amount.

As you enter another room, you'll continue to discover new feelings are awakening deep down inside. And then, all of a sudden, you'll notice the music playing in the background. Has that been playing the entire time? Wow! You're not sure why you're so overwhelmed, but you'll find yourself wanting this new feeling, fantasizing about it. You'll ask yourself, could I recreate this seductive lifestyle and actually feel like this all of the time?

You start taking visual notes: paint, lighting, music, flowers, fabric, and candles ... mustn't forget the candles. You'll tuck away this list of possible new realities in your secret place of dreams and make a personal promise to yourself that from this moment on, it's a new beginning. Even if it's just to add some flowers and an aromatic candle to your bedroom, you will be forever changed.

I'll be there with you.

Moll

Seductive BEGINNINGS

The approach to designing any space is the same, no matter if it's a sprawling mansion, small house, vacation home, apartment, Airstream trailer, or a tent in the woods. Always start with a reason for the space—that is, how you will live in it. Then determine how to create a place that makes you excited to hurry home to it every evening. It doesn't matter which part of the country you live in or if it's specific to a territory. You still have to make your home your special space. It's your place to rest, work, play, eat, entertain, and—most important—romance your partner. So whether you live in a big city or a small town, on the mountaintops of Wyoming or the beaches of South Carolina, you must always bring your vision of excitement and sensuality to a space.

My keys to creating intimate spaces are highlighted throughout *The Seductive Home* journey. My sensory-scape approach is immersed in my keys to fashion, color, texture, scale, lighting, and scent. Each of these seductive homes reveals the keys to my vision, and each is influenced by the colors, textures, and focal points of its surroundings.

Seductive
OLD WORLD

I will never forget the day my husband, Charlie, and I were looking at houses in Knoxville, Tennessee, searching for a place to call "our home." We had looked all day, but not one house spoke to our hearts. There was only one more house on our list to see. I was hopeful and felt that if it were meant to be, then this last stop would be the one. As we pulled into the driveway, Charlie looked at me and said, "You know that I have saved the best for last?" All of a sudden I *knew* that this was going to be the one!

And there it was—a Spanish Mediterranean-style villa more than one hundred years old. Only three families had ever lived in this home. It was perfect. It felt like "home" before we had even stepped inside. If fact, I was so instantly drawn to the house, I don't remember getting out of the car or walking to the door. The house had amazing bones and an incredible history. The great actress Patricia Neal had taken acting classes in the den from Emily Mahan Faust, a brilliant acting coach and daughter of E.C. Mahan, who hired Charles Barber to refashion the original farmhouse into a villa. Emily actually visited when we started construction on the home and walked with us through the house sharing many stories. My favorite was listening to her recall the day she married the love of her life, Hugh Faust, in front of the living room fireplace.

I was hopeful and felt that if it were meant to be, then this last stop would be the one.

Emily returned once the house was finished. It was wonderful to see her so excited and happy to be in her home again and knowing that she loved what we had done with the place. Emily passed away in 2010 at the age of 96. Charlie and I were blessed to have had her visit our home and share her memories with us. That experience will forever be so special in our hearts.

Fashion is not
something that exists
in dresses only.
Fashion is in the sky,
in the street; fashion
has to do with ideas,
the way we live,
what is happening.
—Coco Chanel

17

Sensory—SCAPING

Sensory-scaping: The key to a seductive home is to immerse your surroundings in elements that capture the senses. Create a sensory experience with color, texture, scale, lighting, scent, and dramatic focal points that add the *wow* factor.

There are moments in life when you see something so captivating, it touches your soul. It is this way with art. Sometimes a work of art, whether it's a painting, a photograph, or a sculpture, speaks to you in an indescribable way. This is how I felt the first time I saw the work of David Braly. Charlie and I were at a friend's house the first time I saw one of his exquisite works, and later when I met Charlie's parents, I was touched again to see another David Braly painting that he had personalized for them. As I planned the renovation to our Old World home, I had a vision in my mind where I would place one of his paintings. It is one of the most inspiring pieces in our home. David created a mural of our lives. It's a fabulous work of art that's like a family tree; it symbolizes where we came from and what we are building together. Our home, our children, and someday our grandchildren will be added to the mural.

Why don't you slip out of those wet clothes

and into a dry martini?

—Robert Benchley

A kitchen is the heart of a home, and I *love* our kitchen. My love of open spaces influenced my vision for my homes, and especially my kitchens. I would rather live in one big room than a bunch of small rooms that are much more confining. Opening my kitchen to the adjoining great room made it a more welcoming place for company and brought warmth to my space. Using large-scale pieces and oversized, comfortable furniture helps add to the inviting appeal.

One of my favorite times in the evening is when my husband pulls up a stool to the island counter and joins me in conversation as I'm slicing, chopping, and cooking our dinner. Sharing a glass of wine and the events of the day while we prepare a meal together is something we look forward to. Cooking is a passion of mine and because we travel so often, these quiet times at home together are something we cherish. We may have a seductive dinner for two in front of the fire, or curl up in overstuffed chairs to watch some stress-reducing comedies, but whatever it is, sharing time together at home is a welcome treat.

30

DECADENT
details

The finishing touches are key to adding decadent details to your home. The surfaces and finishes of the walls, floors, counters, and paint selections can turn an ordinary space into an extraordinary, seductive home.

Seductive
BOUDOIR

I'm bringing back the boudoir! Why? Because we all need to set aside a special place in our homes, even if it's only a small space, that's dedicated just to us. Think of it as your personal sanctuary from the chaos of life. I love everything about the idea!

The whole concept of having your very own personal space is sophisticated, peaceful, *and* chic! It doesn't matter whether you're getting ready for work, the gym, grocery store, charity gala, board meeting, car pool—or you might not be leaving the house at all!

A place to sit along with a dressing table and a fabulous mirror to prepare yourself for the day or evening is so sensual. It sets the tone for your day. Listen to your favorite music while you're adding the finishing touches, such as lipstick or exquisite jewelry, tying your silk scarf, applying delectable perfume or cologne, or just taking a moment for yourself to sit quietly in front of the mirror.

> A place to sit along with a dressing table and a fabulous mirror to prepare yourself for the day or evening is so sensual.

You will change how you feel about yourself and your outlook toward life if you take care of yourself and live your best life daily, whatever your "best life" is. You will become a more positive force when you create a ritual to start you on a journey to creating a more seductive home.

38

Today, fashion is really about sensuality—how a woman feels on the inside. In the eighties women used suits with exaggerated shoulders and waists to make a strong impression. Women are now more comfortable with themselves and their bodies— they no longer feel the need to hide behind their clothes.

—Donna Karan

I don't understand how a woman can leave the house

without fixing herself up a little—if only out of politeness.

And then, you never know, maybe that's the day

she has a date with destiny.

And it's best to be as pretty as possible for destiny.

—Coco Chanel

Christian Dior

Know, first, who you are;

then adorn yourself accordingly.

—*Epictetus*

DECADENT *details* 47

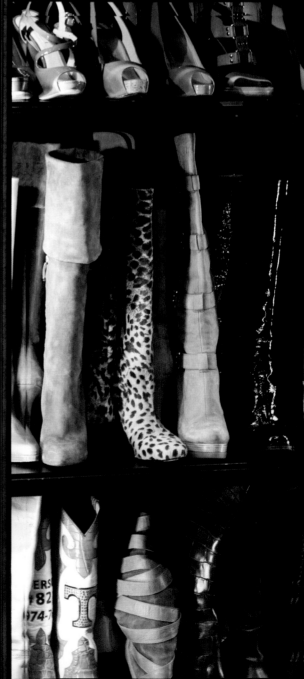

THE ROOM

Have you ever heard the expression "wearing the room"? Subconsciously, you know that your style is reflected not just in your wardrobe but in your home as well. Reflect on what your home and your wardrobe say about you. Are they saying the same thing? To design your home, you need to know who you are, how you dress, how you live, and most important, how you *dream* of living.

To create a seductive lifestyle, you and your home need to be the same. If you want to really know yourself and your style, spend some time in your closet. Your closet tells so many stories about who you really are. At first glance you see fabrics, colors, prints, solids, textures, and the designers you have chosen. You will begin to see the tones of color that are most comfortable for you and that you wear most often. Your wardrobe reveals your personal style.

> To design your home, you need to know who you are, how you dress, how you live, and most important, how you *dream* of living.

If it isn't the style you aspire to, then think about the style you hope to achieve. Experiment with your wardrobe. Go shopping. Explore the possibilities outside your comfort zone. Try on clothes that bring out your inner desires. Take some risks.

Once you develop some confidence with a seductive style, you'll begin to "wear the room." Create a room that reflects your desired style and add elements that bring your style to life!

Ode to Bijan

Accessorize YOUR HOME

Pillow or purse? Tassel or necklace? Throw or scarf?

The key to accessorizing any home is to use the same style sense that makes you uniquely you when you are accessorizing your wardrobe. Home décor accessories are no different than fashion accessories; each adds the finishing touches to the composition. When adding accessories to your outfit, you should stand back and observe yourself in the mirror. What feature do you want to emphasize? What accessory should you add that would provide *wow* to your wardrobe? Is it the shoes, the purse, the jewelry, or a scarf? When you add details to your space, ask yourself these same questions. Where do you want to draw the eye? What elements do you want to emphasize? How will you add that *wow* factor? Where will you add that punch of color, shape, or texture?

> The key to accessorizing any home is to use the same style sense that makes you uniquely you when you are accessorizing your wardrobe.

When dressing, observe yourself from all angles, adjust the lighting, and examine how lighting affects color. Evening lighting requires a richer color palette to bring vibrancy to your makeup and add impact to your wardrobe. Bring it up a notch for evening. Lighting also has an effect on the paint colors in your space. Before choosing paint or fabric for a room, examine the colors in daylight and in evening light. Paint several colors on a wall before you choose the color. You will be amazed how different colors absorb the light.

When accessorizing, try to get an overall feel when you look at the space. Is it bland and underdressed? Is it stunning and well put together? Or is it cluttered? Do you need to edit the room? Do you have too many elements that get lost in the room rather than one or two that makes a statement? Experiment by removing some accent pillows or accessories, and play with the scale of the objects. It's the same when accessorizing your wardrobe. Don't overdo it. Choose one or two accessories that makes a bold statement.

The most exciting part of accessorizing is that every time you find yourself passionate for a special handbag, necklace, scarf, or shoes, whatever it is that speaks *wow* to your senses, remember CPU! That's the "Cost Per Use" of an object. The idea is that you will make great fashion choices if you make sure that it not only speaks to you but also can be used as an accessory to your boudoir! The fun part is that you will find yourself creating vignettes with your beautiful things and you will enjoy them more. Remember that smart choices don't need to be stressful choices ... one beautiful handbag speaks volumes.

Inviting family and friends into our homes as overnight guests is an intimate gift. I love treating guests to an experience that makes them feel as if they are staying at a fine hotel or resort. That means adding just a few touches to welcome them into your home. Fresh flowers in a vase by the bed and warm lighting are easy ways to add a welcoming ambiance to a guest room. Add a couple of chairs and ottomans, if possible, so your guests can escape for a moment of privacy, make an important call, or just steal a quick nap. Internet access is an essential need, so make it easy for your guests by placing a wireless internet card in the room with the password. Every home and every guest are different, but regardless of the size of your guest room, add some comfortable touches to make everyone feel honored.

Guest Suites

Whether you have a very special guest room or a pull-out couch, it's essential to remember that crisp, clean linens are a must. Don't just grab odds-and-ends or mixed-up patterns. When it comes to dressing a guest bed, linens need to match, be freshly laundered, and look inviting. Think simple and elegant when choosing your linens; nothing beats a set of freshly ironed white sheets. Don't forget to offer blankets even if it's the middle of summer. Everyone has a different body temperature. We keep our house very cool at night (perfect for us). Always remember to be thoughtful and have some kind of easy-to-find blanket or throw, just in case.

Pillows and duvets can also be another opportunity to offer hospitality when it comes to comfort. I *love* goose down but you should provide a synthetic option just in case a guest has allergies. You can avoid this situation simply by checking with your guests ahead of time and having suitable choices on hand. (Don't forget to ask about food allergies as well; it can save you from a long night in the

I love hideaways, and my Old World home in Knoxville had the perfect place to create a hideaway to get away, cuddle up, or watch an old movie together with my husband, Charlie. This room was nothing more than an office with a door, separated from everything else in the house. It's located in the middle of the stair landing and didn't work as a bedroom. I decided it would be a perfect place to create a media room for the guest quarters.

I removed the door and created an archway. The hand-applied painting around the doorway makes it extra special, especially with the seventeenth-century Italian sconces. The walls are padded in faux leather in a lizard green color. It is so cool! I added three twin-sized sofas fashioned into a sleek sectional lining the walls. The cushions are teddy bear mohair in a perfect color match to the sofas. Now the room has lovingly been named "The Lizard Lounge." It is the perfect space for our kids to hang out in and the adults to steal away to.

70

Life is not measured by the number of breaths we take,
but by the moments that take our breath away.

—unknown

It's the same seduction that one first feels when touching cashmere or fur ... Nobody touches fur once, or cashmere once. With wine, you want to keep it in your mouth, you want to play with it, you want to roll it around until you get it.

— Joshua Wesson

74

Give me a laundry list
and I'll set it to music.
—Gioacchino Rossini

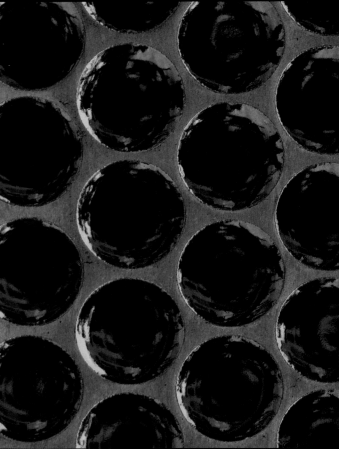

DECADENT
details

All architecture is shelter,
all great architecture is the design of space
that contains, cuddles, exalts, or
stimulates the persons in that space.
—Philip Johnson

There is a fountain of youth: it is in your mind, your talents, the creativity you bring to your life and the lives of people you love. When you learn to tap this source, you will have truly defeated age.

—Sophia Loren

Seductive
MODERN CITY

Welcome to our loft in downtown Nashville, Tennessee. Now, most of you might not consider Nashville "big city living." But while it may not be New York or Los Angeles, it has a big city vibe with a charming, small town feel. You just cannot help but fall in love with this city. It's a very special place to live. Our Inspiration Destination for our loft was the Mandarin Oriental Hotel in New York City. My husband, Charlie, and I eloped on March 18, 2006, and celebrated with a few close friends in the Presidential Suite. With such wonderful memories we now lovingly refer to our city home as "Mandarin South."

With such wonderful memories we now lovingly refer to our city home as "Mandarin South."

"Music City USA"—talk about a city that seduces you! Oh yes, Nashville! Everywhere you turn, music is seducing many passionate hearts. Nashville is also one of the friendliest towns I have ever known. I moved here in July 1999. It was an amazing feeling to pick up and completely change my life as I moved thousands of miles away from Scottsdale, Arizona, and all that was familiar to me. Nothing about these two cities was similar in any way. Scottsdale is lovely in its own charming way, but it's very brown and flat. You can look across the valley and see exactly where you're heading. It's a well-planned community with gorgeous manicured greenbelts right in the middle of a desert.

Nashville welcomed me with completely new terrain where everything was green and lush but was so dense it was seemingly more difficult to navigate. The weather was completely different as well. I went from dry to unbelievably humid conditions. And oh yes, winter! I had never lived in a location that experienced all four seasons. I have learned to absolutely adore fall, winter, and our spectacular spring. I left summer out on purpose.

The house does not frame the view:
It projects the beholder into it.
—Harwell Hamilton Harris

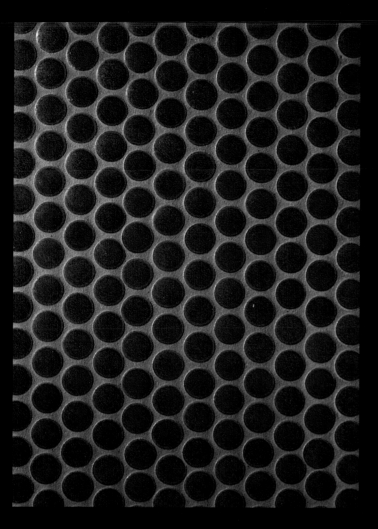

DECADENT *details*

Art is the window to man's soul.
Without it, he would never be able to see beyond his
immediate world; nor could the world see the man within.
—Lady Bird Johnson

Adornment is never anything except
a reflection of the heart.

—Coco Chanel

A touch of the unexpected in a guest room makes a stay in your home memorable. For this guest room, I used my favorite color scheme of black and white. Why? Because it's strong, shocking, unexpected, and extremely sophisticated. It makes a great *wow* statement. I added the keys to sensory-scaping the room with eye-catching focal points, a mix of textures, candles, and lighting. It's so satisfying as a hostess to see the reactions of our overnight guests when they see their guest rooms, and this room leaves our guests with an unforgettable experience. The greatest compliment possible is when we host a party and I hear guests or family giving a tour and saying, "You've got to see my room; this is where I stay when I visit!"

I added the keys to sensory-scaping the room with eye-catching focal points, a mix of textures, candles, and lighting.

Seductive
SOUTHWEST

A seductive Santa Fe sunset sets my soul on fire. After growing up in Scottsdale, Arizona, then living in several different places throughout my life, there was a part of me that missed the majestic desert. I began visiting Santa Fe years ago and it quickly became a place I knew I would always go back to. I took my husband, Charlie, one year to celebrate the Fourth of July; he instantly shared my love for the city, so we chose to buy a home there.

A seductive Santa Fe sunset sets my soul on fire.

When I first met the previous owner of our Santa Fe home, Doug Atwill, I was blown away with his huge spirit and by the joy he exuded. His home matched his personality and had the same amazing energy. It was very seductive—he had created an artist's hideaway tucked back behind a weathered gate and lush gardens. My husband and I entered our soon-to-be Santa Fe home not knowing what to expect. As we walked through the doors for the first time, I couldn't help but notice the living room boasting an easel with a half-finished canvas on it; the owner had been painting just hours before we arrived. The kitchen was in full swing, with pots flying out of the cupboards and food artfully being prepared for a friendly gathering later in the evening. It was so cool. I knew at that moment that this was the Southwest retreat for Charlie and me.

I wanted to keep my home as authentic to the area as possible, but with my own seductive twist, of course. Because New Mexico isn't just around the corner from our home in Tennessee, it was much easier to buy all of the basics locally. To include the flavor of Santa Fe, I shopped for accessories and art once I arrived. I found some of my favorite items at flea markets, consignment stores, and unique shops in town.

I love the new home we created in Santa Fe; when I am there, I can feel the energy that is unique to this special town the second I walk through our front gate. Spending time here is my way of unwinding and staying connected to my husband, friends, loved ones, and the things that inspire me. I guess you could call Santa Fe my "Inspiration Destination." Your home—the place of your refuge—reflects who you are. Is it where you want to be? If not, what are you waiting for?

Casa De ChaMoll SANTA FE, NEW MEXICO

*There is not enough darkness in all the world
to put out the light of even one small candle.*

—Robert Alden

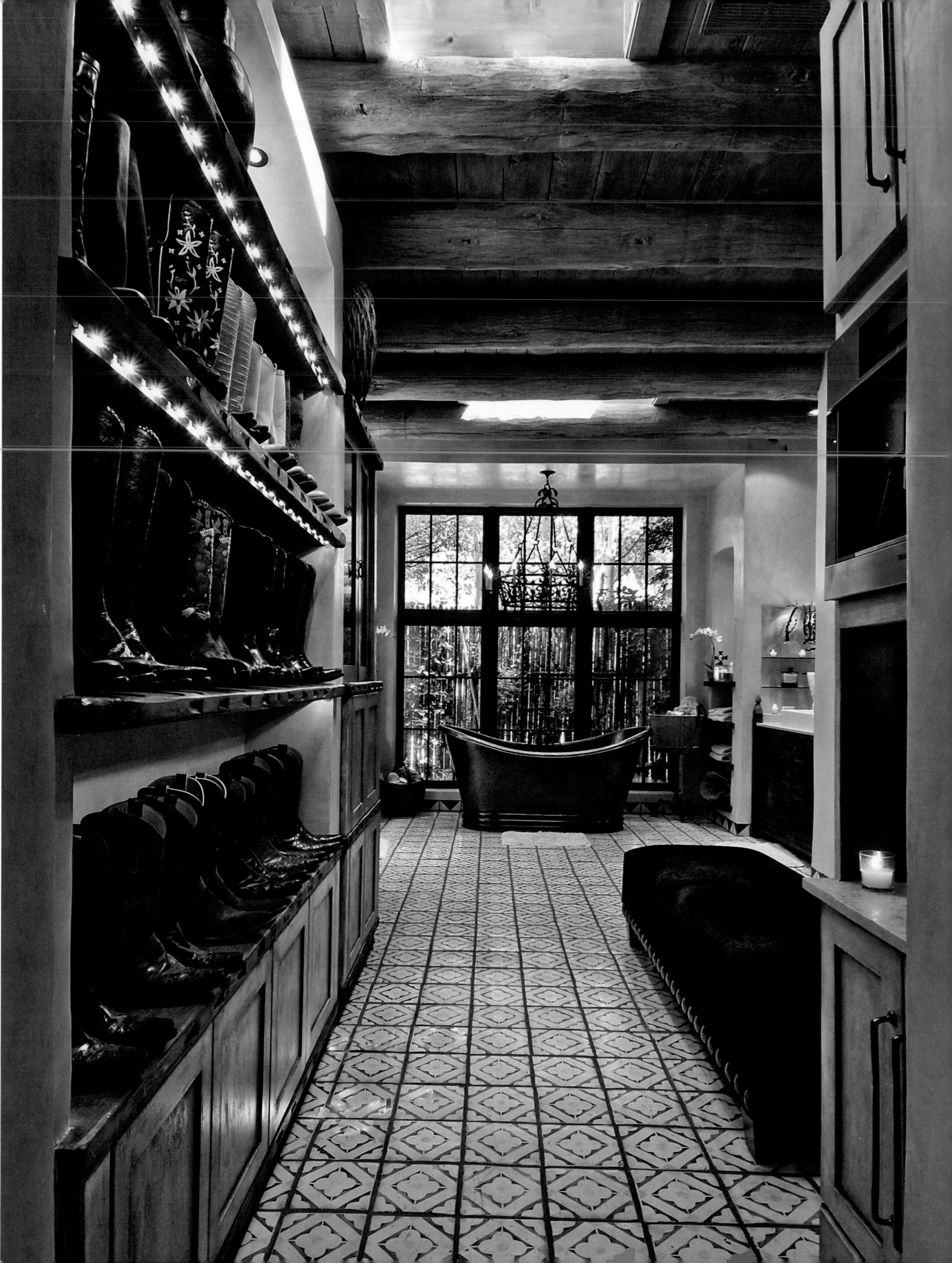

There's nothing seductive about doing the laundry, but it's certainly necessary. So if you don't have the space to create a pretty laundry room then by all means hide it!   —Moll

120

DECADENT
details

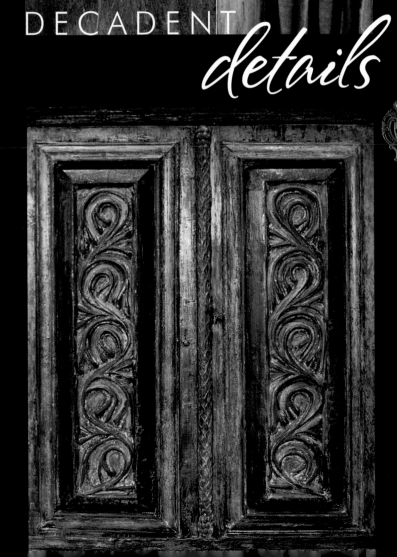

Come, south wind recalling love. Breathe on my garden,
let aromas swell in the air, my love will graze among the flowers.

—St. John of the Cross

Every house where love abides
And friendship is a guest,
Is surely home, and home, sweet home
For there the heart can rest.

—Henry van Dyke

Sensory-scaping is about the "wow factor" —
creating seductive focal points that capture your imagination!

Seductive ENTERTAINING

The key to achieving any seductive setting is the same whether you're entertaining one guest, your family, or hundreds. You must create a setting that speaks to your passions, a setting that will transport you and your guests to a full sensory experience. I have always been passionate about my space even when my wallet was less than abundant. Luckily, creating ambiance is absolutely achievable without exceeding your budget. I was on a strict budget at different times in my life, and it was during those times that I designed some of the most amazing and unique table settings and rooms. I had to dig deep to find creative ways to achieve a seductive home on a tight budget. It's a lot of fun to run wild inside your imagination as you unlock your inner seductive side.

The key to achieving any seductive setting is the same whether you're entertaining one guest, your family, or hundreds.

Remember that you are not only creating wonderful memories but that you are giving a special gift to others by opening your home. Entertaining in your home is always special, but entertaining in a seductive home is inspiring. You will inspire others to start searching inside themselves to find their own inspirations to seductive entertaining. You will become part of a powerful movement to bring people back to what's important—the home.

There's nothing like an evening under the stars in your very own backyard! It's *the* most elegant and sensual backdrop one could ever choose for a gala gathering of many guests or an intimate dinner at a table for two. The sky is the limit when it comes to your imagination. Your inspiration can come from anywhere—maybe it's the amazing travels you've physically experienced, or the meditative trips you've taken while perusing travel magazines. Maybe it's from watching romantic films that take place in luxurious and magical settings. Simply let a captivating destination lead you on a journey to recreate a similar, seductive atmosphere in your own way and within your budget.

*There's nothing sexier than a woman
        who is comfortable in her own shoes.*
                            —unknown

One should either be a work of art, or wear a work of art.

—Oscar Wilde

I love planning an event for my family and friends. It's truly a joy to look for new and exciting ways to amaze people. I approach planning a party just as I do when I start to design a room. The key is always to start with an element that speaks to you and let it lead you in your inspired direction. Sometimes I start with an incredible large-scale piece of art that blows me away or an undeniably beautiful old rug as the foundation of a space.

The key is always to start with an element that speaks to you and let it lead you in your inspired direction.

For a party, sometimes it's as simple as falling in love with a dress that makes me feel great, makes me smile. Before I know it, I have a theme. Standing in Donna Karan in New York, I slipped into this fabulous red dress and that was it; I said, "We will make it 'An Evening in Red'." The "it" was a fundraiser for Habitat for Humanity. Sometimes it's a theme that seems to transport you and your guests to another country, or if it's a party for someone special, it might have a vibe that's undeniably them. It's so fun to create an evening that allows people to reach beyond themselves and enjoy pushing the envelope. When it's for an amazing charity like Habitat for Humanity, it is easy to go for it and make it happen. It's inspiring when your guests participate and lose themselves in the magic of the evening as well as join in raising a lot of money for a cause.

Seductive
HOSTESS

If you can dream it, anything is possible! If you can visualize a feeling and make it literally come to life, then you have mastered the art of entertaining. There are many levels of entertaining guests. Sometimes it's making an old family recipe that's a "can't miss" with your children, or something simple like grilling burgers. Maybe it's planning formal dinners with a chef or picking up some take-out food and placing it on that exquisitely patterned china you never pull out of the cabinet. Sometimes it's the most unexpected moments you remember. Those evenings when, with no notice at all, you still pull off a party perfectly. It's those special times that go down in the memory books for years to come. What was it that sets those evenings apart? I call it being party ready! Being party ready allows you to gracefully pull out those must-haves you have tucked in your pantry for moments just like this, such as the wine you keep stashed away "just in case." It's having a bar set up like the one we use as a fabulous accent, in a room that begs for entertaining. When you're a "seductive hostess" you're always "party ready" for any impromptu gathering.

A seductive hostess is prepared for absolutely anything.

That's the secret to any seductive hostess! A seductive hostess is prepared for absolutely anything. It helps to have a few failsafe, tried-and-true, stunning cocktail outfits to fit just about any level of entertaining, from picnics to black tie. Don't wait until you *need* a hostess wardrobe to get one, though. If you plan ahead there will be no stress. Trust me, there is nothing worse than waiting until the last minute to figure out what you're wearing. My personal must-haves are simple metallic flats or my favorite pair of Louboutin's I can slip into with jeans and a little sequin tank. Black Capri pants are a must, with a few options of tops so you can dress up or down according to the occasion. Some slinky little cocktail dresses and a simple long black gown are so easy to accessorize. Alterations are a must; your outfit doesn't have to cost a fortune, but it does need to fit properly. Hair should always be pulled away from your face— think chignon. When I'm in a hurry I always go for a high ponytail; it's easy, sophisticated, and it keeps my hair out of the way (it also takes a few years off any seasoned hostess).

The idea is to actually enjoy entertaining! If *you're* not having fun, no one else will either. So let go and become a seductive hostess who exudes joy and a welcoming warmth to friends and family every time they enter your home.

Ravioli with Butter Sage Sauce

Fresh, store-bought ravioli of your choice

1 stick butter

6 fresh sage leaves, coarsely chopped,
plus more for garnish

½ tsp. minced garlic

Sea salt, to taste

Fresh-ground black pepper, to taste

Fresh Parmesan cheese

Cook the ravioli according to package directions. Combine the butter with the chopped sage, garlic, salt, and pepper in a microwave-safe bowl. Cover and microwave on high for 2 minutes. Immediately pour the sauce over the ravioli. Toss some fresh sage leaves on top, sprinkle some Parmesan cheese, and *Buon Appetito!* Serves 4.

Seductive
TABLES FOR TWO

The dining experience is one of the most important keys in family life and entertaining. Most homes have a designated dining table that can seat at least six people; some can even seat eight or more. But sometimes when it is just the two of you, a table that size seems like a vast area that leaves you feeling less than cozy. If sitting at opposite ends of a large table is not your style, then creating another place for two is a wonderful thing (and I am not talking TV tray tables in front of the television).

My husband and I love our great room because it's open to our kitchen, dining, and television room. But, we also have this very long table that can seat twelve comfortably and sometimes even more than that. One night, though, I became frustrated with having a less-than-intimate table, so I went on a scavenger hunt to solve this problem. I zeroed in on a small, round table from the formal living area, and carried it into the great room. I then pulled up two chairs to face the table, and *voila*! There it was, a seductive table for two.

The dining experience is one of the most important keys in family life and entertaining.

This was the best design decision I ever made for that room, mostly because it carved out a space for just the two of us. This intimate space is what *everyone* comments about when they enter that room. You can't miss it. It's very seductive! A simple meal, shared in an intimate space, is such a wonderful way to your significant other's heart.

Moll's Bean Soup

1 HoneyBaked® ham bone

6 cups cold water

6 cups prepared vegetable broth

1 package HoneyBaked® Ham Bone
  Soup Mix

1 Tbsp. butter

2 bay leaves

1 28-oz. can whole tomatoes

1 cup diced celery

1 cup diced onions

2 tsp. chopped garlic

1 tsp. ground pepper

$\frac{1}{2}$ tsp. ground sea salt

1 tsp. ground Chophouse Blend from
  Fresh Market

Crostini

2 Tbsp. olive oil

Balsamic vinegar

Fresh Parmesan cheese, grated

■ Place the ham bone in large stockpot and add the water and stock;
bring to a boil. Add the contents of the soup mix seasoning packet.
Return the ham and liquids to a boil, then reduce heat and simmer
approximately 2 hours. Place the butter, bay leaves, tomatoes, celery,
onion, garlic, pepper, salt, and Chophouse Blend into a large sauté
pan and sauté lightly. Set aside. Remove the ham bone and allow it to
cool. Add the sautéed vegetables and beans from the soup mix to the
liquid in the stockpot and cook over moderate heat for approximately
1 hour, or until the beans from the soup mix are tender. Remove the
meat from the ham bone and dice; add to the soup and mix well.
Remove 6 cups of the soup and place into kitchen blender. Cover
and purée. Pour the purée back into the large pot of soup.

■ Serve with the crostini. Drizzle with the olive oil and balsamic vinegar,
and top with the Parmesan cheese. Serves 4 to 6.

Impromptu TABLES FOR TWO

What's your idea of a power lunch? Some people would say that there's only one kind, but I believe that there are two. One is strictly business; those can be held at a restaurant, an office, or a boardroom. But there's another kind of power lunch—the impromptu lunch for two. These impromptu moments are about a couple connecting over the most powerful lunch of all—an unexpected, uninterrupted lunch spent together.

These impromptu moments are about a couple connecting over the most powerful lunch of all— an unexpected, uninterrupted lunch spent together.

Think about this scenario: Your partner calls and wants to meet you for lunch, so you suggest grabbing a bite at home. Why not? The weather is incredibly beautiful today, so you run home and slip out of your business suit or jeans and slip into a dress that you've been dying to wear. Then you create the perfect romantic lunch scenario. Remember that this is your dream lunch. Use whatever is available to you at home. I love dishes, china, crystal, and linens, so I collect a mix of pieces. I absolutely use everything I collect. I often buy sets of two of everything, such as cups, dishes, placemats, napkins, and so forth. It's affordable, and with the great selections that can be found at many stores, you can have many choices on hand to choose from for these impromptu meals for two.

Cobb Salad Tower

1 lb. deli chicken (sliced thick and cubed in ½-inch cubes)

10 slices bacon, chopped (precooked works great!)

¼ cup plus 1 tsp. bleu cheese dressing

¼ cup bleu cheese crumbles

¼ tsp. fresh-ground black pepper

1 large head romaine lettuce, shredded

1½ Tbsp. white wine vinaigrette

4 Roma or plum tomatoes, thinly sliced

⅛ tsp. salt

1 avocado, peeled and thinly sliced (reserve half)

- Place the chicken in a small bowl and add the bacon. Stir in the bleu cheese dressing, crumbles, and pepper. Set aside. Place the romaine in a large bowl. Toss with the vinaigrette. Sprinkle the tomatoes with the salt.

- To make the tower, rinse a 14 oz. can (a fruit or vegetable can is great), opened on both ends. It's going to be a mold for the salad. Place the can on a plate and layer the ingredients. Start by packing a handful of the romaine in the bottom, then arrange 3 or 4 slices of the tomato over the lettuce. Top that with a couple of pieces of avocado. Scoop ⅓ cup of the chicken, bacon, and bleu cheese mixture and place on top of the avocado. Using the back of a spoon, or the flat part of a measuring cup, press down (firmly) to make everything compact. Add another small handful of lettuce and another layer of tomatoes. Press down once again to make it compact. Slowly remove the can from the salad. The lettuce on the bottom will spread out, but everything else should remain layered. Garnish with a few slices of avocado on the top and a few bleu cheese crumbles around the plate. Serves 4.

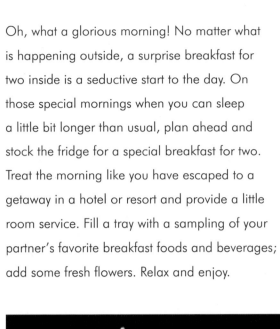

Oh, what a glorious morning! No matter what is happening outside, a surprise breakfast for two inside is a seductive start to the day. On those special mornings when you can sleep a little bit longer than usual, plan ahead and stock the fridge for a special breakfast for two. Treat the morning like you have escaped to a getaway in a hotel or resort and provide a little room service. Fill a tray with a sampling of your partner's favorite breakfast foods and beverages; add some fresh flowers. Relax and enjoy.

Charlie's Pasta

2 Tbsp. olive oil

6 cloves garlic, coarsely chopped

1 red bell pepper, sliced into strips

1 orange bell pepper, sliced into strips

8 oz. package sliced mushrooms

Cayenne pepper

Sea salt

Fresh-ground black pepper

8.8 oz. jar sun-dried tomato pesto

28 oz. can tomatoes, drained

1 jar red pasta sauce (pick your favorite)

3 large basil leaves, torn into strips, plus more
    for garnish

1 handful (about 15) pitted Kalamata olives

6 oz. jar artichoke hearts, drained

1 lb. penne pasta

Roast chicken breast meat, shredded

Parmesan cheese

- In a large sauté pan, heat the olive oil over medium-high heat. When the oil is hot, add the garlic and sauté 1 minute. If the garlic starts to brown, reduce the heat. Add the bell peppers and toss well. Cover the pan and cook for 2 minutes. Uncover; add the mushrooms and a pinch of cayenne pepper (or to taste). Season with the salt and pepper, and cook for 1 minute. Reduce the heat to medium-low.

- Add the pesto, tomatoes, pasta sauce, basil, olives, and artichoke hearts. Let the sauce simmer gently while you cook the pasta (prepare according to package directions). As the pasta finishes cooking, add the chicken to the sauce to heat through. Drain the pasta and put into a large bowl. Add the sauce and toss to combine. Serve immediately, topped with the Parmesan cheese and basil. Serves 4 to 6.

Tip: When using a whole roast chicken, you can always save the drumsticks for the kids'
or your lunch the next day!

One key to spicing up romance is to add an element of surprise. Bringing in a touch of the unexpected to an ordinary experience is one way to invite intimacy. I like discovering intimate settings in my home for special dinners for two. Surprise yourself. Think beyond how you use your existing space. Or better yet, expand your living space to the outdoors and use the ambiance of the evening light and a little candlelight for a romantic dinner for

One key to spicing up romance is to add an element of surprise.

two. Starlit nights will disguise any unsightly patio furniture or overgrown lawns, but more important, it sets the mood for a seductive night with your significant other. Have fun with the experience! Set your table with what you have. Bring out the china and crystal and dress it up with flowers and candles. No matter what you use to create your table for two, the experience will be unforgettable.

Coming up with new and exciting ways to serve a last-minute meal for my husband is actually fun for me. One particular afternoon we both had worked long hours, and we forgot completely about dinner. I wanted to do something special so I raced home ahead of my husband. I ran to the refrigerator in search of something, *anything*, I could throw together. Literally all that we had were frozen dinners (three Lean Cuisine meals to be exact); one was cheddar potatoes with broccoli and two were Swedish meatballs with fettuccine. Meatballs it was. So, I put my "presentation is everything" skills to the test, and decided that maybe we would visit Morocco for dinner. I used Italian parsley, a sprinkle of goat cheese, cracked pepper, paprika, and cayenne pepper to dress the plate. Thank heaven for my Naeem Khan dress, my fabulous Tibetan doors, a couple of palms, a table and chairs from the house, and some gorgeous china and crystal. It was a real stretch, but I made it work, and off to Marrakech we went!

▲ *after*

before ▶

Seductive
TRANSFORMATIONS

The key to transforming your space is first to have the courage to make a change. Create a picture in your mind of each space and imagine how you want the room to function, and then imagine how you want the room to feel, and most important, how the room and your home will reflect who you are and how you want to live. Within each space lie endless possibilities. Don't be afraid to get started.

The key to transforming your space is first to have the courage to make a change.

As a designer, I am able to visualize the finished space from the moment I walk into a room. I didn't realize at first that this was not something everyone can do, but now I understand that what may be natural for me may take a little more inspiration for others. So I have included the transformation pictures of each home in the final pages of this book. The before and after, and sometimes the in-between, pictures reveal the evolution of each space from start to finish. I hope that these snapshots of my journey will inspire you to discover the possibilities in your own home. Each person is unique, each home is unique, and finding the inspiration to make *your* home uniquely yours is within you.

If nothing ever changed, there'd be no butterflies.

—unknown

▲ *before* ▶

This was a beautiful old house that needed a lot of love and attention to bring its best features back to life. It was totally charming, yet the more time we spent living in it, the more we realized we needed to change it to fit our family's needs.

Sometimes, if you take your time to listen, old houses will speak to you, and you just may uncover lost treasures like we found around our front door. There, underneath many years of white high-gloss enamel paint, we found *beautiful* stonework. One day we chipped a bit of the paint off and it was like being on an incredible archeological dig. To bring our home's exterior back to life we removed a window, added a new roof, brought in lots of stone for a new terrace and walkway, hung new shutters and awnings, and added a bit of landscaping. *Voila*! We had a beautiful home with seductive, Old World charm.

If at all possible, spend some time in any newly acquired old space before you make any decisions and draw up architectural plans. That is the only way you will really know what you need to fix, add, or replace.

▲ *after* ▶

before

before ▶

after

after

The addition of the terrace (above right) corrected a dangerous hazard. Originally the house had a covered porch terrace that faced the gardens. Over the years, additions and remodels had taken place, and the porch had become a beautiful Florida room. Unfortunately, the stairs could still be accessed from the Florida room doors with no way to stop guests from falling out the middle door. So we solved that problem by adding a terrace, which has become a wonderful place to dine. This side view of the house shows the addition and where we married the old part of the home with the new part. I have to give Ron Hutchins (my design architect) a huge shout-out because our roofline is spectacular; when you walk around the entire house the design is seamless. Blending the old with the new is truly the most difficult part of any restoration.

before

new addition work in progress

after

before   after ▼

189

before

Sometimes a picture speaks a thousand words! This was the original pool and pool area in three different stages. We kept the original pool but gutted it and added new plumbing. The inside surface of the pool bottom was darkened and a blue-bottom pebble tech was added to give the pool a sexy lagoon look and vibe. My inspiration for this pool, if you're old enough to remember, was the famous Chanel No. 5 commercial with the swimming pool. If you don't remember it, trust me, it was *awesome*. My own twist was adding the wall and the architectural piece at the end. As you can see, it was still lacking a focal point, so I asked artist Mark Montoya to paint between the arches. By adding full-sized mattresses on wrought-iron stands, pillows, and lighting, we now have a seductive poolside setting.

after

All the great old homes and estates have a lanai or a sexy cabana lounge area. So of course a seductive home begs for any place you can create a hideaway. I wanted to create one to escape from the sun on a hot afternoon and also to have a spot to dangle my feet in the water. With deep, low steps extending from the pool, our lanai makes these wishes possible. I added two water features and placed urns on either side. A large built-in sofa, mirrored on the top half, gives the illusion of another patio on the other side. Two wonderful old Tibetan columns were included. The addition of candles and speakers for music *everywhere* completes this sensory-scaped pool area.

The addition of candles and speakers for music *everywhere* completes this sensory-scaped pool area.

after

These two angels pictured are ones that I found that were said to be part of the old family estate of the founders of Morton Salt. They are so spectacular when you see them in person! Even when they sat half opened in their crates, they commanded such a beautiful, spiritual presence that no one could walk by them without reacting. Some workers were almost in prayerful awe. The effect made such an impression on Charlie and me that we named them. Grace and Gabriel.

We love angels, and we collect them from all over the world; so when it was time to resurrect our gardens, the angels became our inspiration. The effect was so peaceful we decided to name our home Casa Di Angeli, meaning "House of Angels."

▲*before*   *after* ▼

▲before

after ▶

before ◀

after ▼

▲ *after*

before ▶

196

▲ *before*   *after* ▼

This building was the original Bellsouth building on the edge of downtown Nashville, so the location was perfect for us. When I first walked into this space it was practically all open, which is why we have only a few before and after pictures. The layout wasn't functional and, to make this *more* complicated, the space was originally configured for office space. But what couldn't be denied were the incredible, unobstructed views of Nashville. The floors and ceiling were concrete, so designing the space meant I had to bring the ceiling down just enough to add lighting and wiring, and raise the floor in order to add new plumbing.

Raising the floor gave me an opportunity to create different levels of staging for sensory-scaping my home. We kept the original bricks across the window walls but updated them with a slate metallic paint for a sleek vibe.   My "wear the room" philosophy was inspired in this space by my husband's wardrobe. The couches were covered with a handsome cognac-colored mohair that reminded me of one of his overcoats. The occasional chairs were inspired by a favorite Tom Ford steel grey suit, and the accents of hot green and burnt orange added the perfect pop of color to the room, much like the perfect tie and pocket scarf top off a man's ensemble.

My "wear the room" philosophy was inspired
in this space by my husband's wardrobe.

▲*before*   *after* ▼

before

after ▶

We started by gutting the entire space. Once it was wide open I wanted to design the loft so that the entertaining areas had the primary front and side window views. I also didn't want to lose the room's open feeling. It made perfect sense to incorporate the living room, dining room, kitchen, and seating area into one large, open space, which allows great traffic flow. This space can easily be rearranged to accommodate large groups for an event or to create more intimate seating arrangements.

The kitchen was fun to plan and I knew exactly what I wanted from the start. The modern city feel is echoed in the kitchen accents, with steel and aluminum as the theme. Pots, pans, and incredible knives provide the cool accents and are the perfect accessories to this gourmet kitchen. The huge island houses a 50-inch plasma television on the front of it so the kitchen seating would be comfortable and relaxing. I placed the icemaker and drawers on the opposite side of the island so they would be accessible. The kitchen counters are topped with sleek black granite that shines like a modern sports car.

▲ *before*

after ▶

The opposite end of this space had an amazing view of downtown Nashville so it was the perfect spot to locate the master bedroom and bath. We wanted this part of the loft to feel completely different and yet sophisticated like the rest of the space. My inspiration was very old Hollywood with Venetian plaster walls that glisten like pearls. The tones of beige were inspired by the La Perla negligee and robe I wore on my honeymoon. I staged the bed for a grand statement, adding accent pillows made from metallic fabric on top of the Frette bedding draped with a beige faux fur

◀ *before*

after ▼

This is the *wow* room that truly blows everyone away. It still blows us away to this day, and that's the truest test of design to me! The hand-cut, dark chocolate-colored teenie-tiny tiles across the entire floor and back wall are my ode to Art Deco! The matching sinks are cut crystal and light up from underneath the cabinets. The tub—that unbelievable soaking tub—is incredibly seductive at night with the lights dimmed, candles lit, and the city view! The dressing table is positioned for perfect lighting to apply makeup and for watching the sun go down while applying the last touches before an evening out.

The drapes didn't need to be completely opaque, but sheers by themselves would not have provided enough privacy. By doubling the fabric, we were able to achieve privacy and not lose the soft, draping, scarflike quality. This chic and fashionable look reminds me of Grace Kelly with her signature sunglasses and long, beautiful scarf blowing in the wind.

▲*before   after* ▼

before

after

◀ before

after ▼

204

after ▲
◀ *before*

Whether you are decorating just one room or an entire house, it's a good idea to create a reference guide to help while you shop for those special pieces. When I began renovating my Santa Fe home, I needed some way to stay organized and cut down on the chaos of trying to decorate a second home while living at my permanent home in Tennessee. I took "before" and "during" pictures of my Santa Fe home and printed them on full-sized sheets of paper on my home printer. Then I organized the shots in a notebook, separating all the photos by each room. I wrote any notes that would help on each picture, including all measurements and items that I needed to get for a particular room. When I was out around town and ran into a great little store, I could pull out my notebook and not only see the space I had to work with, but I also knew its exact measurements and dimensions for any new items I might discover. I had a place in the notebook to keep all receipts and business cards for any of the wonderful new places I stumbled upon during my search. I also took

◀ *before*

after ▼

before
after

before
after

◄ before ▲

▼ after

◄ *before*

▼ *after*

▲ *before*

after ►

before

after

When renovating your home, the most important thing is to hire a great contractor. A competent, licensed contractor becomes your partner to realizing your vision. Having a skilled, trustworthy contractor also reduces your stress during construction in your home. Before choosing one, check their references and take the time to look at work they have done.

▲*before*   *after* ▼

before   *after* ▲

▲*before*   *after* ▼

Transformation is a key to making a space truly yours. This outdoor living space (as seen in this before picture) was wonderful just the way it was, but I wanted to make it perfect for our family. Unfortunately, we had to give up the garden and some of the natural vegetation in order to add more outdoor leisure space for our large family.

Transformation is a key to making a space truly yours.

▲*before*   *after* ▼

215

before

Outdoor spaces provide an opportunity to create a seductive, resort-like atmosphere. Imagine your favorite getaway location and bring those elements to your outdoor living rooms. You don't need to spend a lot of money to make an impact. Here, I wanted to bring a southwestern flair to my patio. I transformed rusty, white wrought-iron chairs with cobalt blue spray paint, which added a surprising burst of southwestern color. The statue received an artist's touch to match the other architectural pieces. I then layered textures with a few pillows to soften the space and add comforting elements to the contrasting hard surfaces. For very little money I created "Casa De ChaMoll."

after

▲*before*   *after* ▼

This guesthouse was a needed addition to our property because the main house has only one bedroom with a casita. Between my husband, Charlie, and me, we have four children, and two of them are now married. The possibility of increasing our family by two more spouses and future grandchildren meant we needed more space. When the house next door became available it made sense for us to buy it. We took the wall down between the two houses and removed two interior walls. Then we removed the brick floors and replaced them with poured stained concrete using the same color scheme as the main house. The ceiling and hardware treatments were duplicated from our southwestern retreat. Finally, the front door of the guesthouse was moved to the courtyard, creating a cozy family haven.

▲*before*   *after* ▼

221

Acknowledgements

If I listed everyone who helped me to create these homes it would be a huge book of amazing and talented people all by itself. Thank you to everyone who made my life easier during these transformation processes and for the talents you contributed to the beauty of our homes.

— *Moll*

222

SEDUCTIVE OLD WORLD

Ron Hutchins and Chris Joice – *architectural design* • **Hickory Construction, Pat Adair, Mike Salley** • **Design Works, Bobbie McCloud** • **Deb Staver, Rose Arnold** – *wall finishes* • **McGaha Electric** • **Marvin Windows & Doors** • **Martin Armendariz** – *custom woodwork* • **Preston Fairbow** – *wine cellar gates, awning spears* • **Kings Custom Hardwood & Steve Burns** • **Elite Millworks, Tom Richardson** – *kitchen* • **McGilveray Woodworks** – *master bedroom and closet* • **David Braly** – *artist, master bathroom ceiling* • **Devol Millwork** – *specialty doors & windows* • **Jay Sutton** – *granite* • **Stone Craft** – *custom stone fireplaces* • **Frank Sutherland** – *wine cellar* • **Renaissance Tile & Bath** – *sinks, faucets, and all tile* • **Herndon & Merry** – *gates and wrought iron, exterior* • **Dennis Jessee** – *all stone work outdoors* • **Ben Page & Associates** – *landscape design* • **Thress Nursery** – *landscape design* • **Price Landscape & Design** • **Tipton Pools** • **Nightscape Design** – *exterior lighting* • **Edwards Plumbing** • **Stanley Best HVAC** • **Juan Valedez Roofing** • **Garland Painting** • **Mike Pizzalongo** – *ceiling work* • **Viking** – *appliances* • **Miele** – *coffee maker* • **Ken, Persian Rug Gallery, Nashville** • **Art de Mexico** • **Rick & Robert, Bennett Galleries & Co** • **Merri Lee, Gift Gourmet & Interiors** • **Michael Peters Home** • **LAWS Interiors** • **Lyons View Gallery** • **Lowe Gallery, Atlanta** • **Fischbach Gallery, New York** • **Meyer East Gallery, Santa Fe** • **McLarry Fine Art Gallery, Santa Fe** • **Gebert Contemporary Gallery, Santa Fe** • **Artifacts, Nashville** • **Recreations, Nashville** • **Sprintz**

SEDUCTIVE MODERN CITY

Kent McTaggert – *contractor* • **Design Works, Bobbie McCloud** • **Deb Staver, Rose Arnold** – *wall finishes* • **Renaissance Tile & Bath** – *all tile, bath, and fixtures* • **Kurt McKeithan** – *kitchen and closet cabinetry* • **Andrew Denny, Textures Flooring** – *bamboo flooring* • **Davishire** • **Ephiany** • **Sprintz** • **Recreations** • **Wolf** – *appliances* • **Miele** – *coffee maker*

SEDUCTIVE SOUTHWEST

Fritz Staver, Staver Builders • Doug Atwill – *architect* • Tim Curry – *architect (guest house)* • Eric J. Montoya, Sierra Vista Electric • Nathan K. Dailey • Abigail Ryan – *wall and wood finishes* • Bobbie McCloud, Design Works • Santa Fe by Design – *sinks, tubs, and plumbing fixtures* • Statements, Santa Fe – *all tile* • David Gallegos – *cabinetry* • Rich Olein, Stonefish – *all countertops* • Guy Dominguez – *all painting* • Elizabeth Robechek & Kristin Erchinger, Clemens & Associates – *landscape design* • Viking – *appliances* • Miele – *coffee maker* • Maytag – *my favorite washer and dryer* • Seret & Sons – *architectural pieces* • Recollections Fine Consignment, Santa Fe • The Ann Lawrence Collection, Santa Fe • Jackalope, Santa Fe • Nashville Persian Rug Gallery, Nashville • Antique Warehouse, Santa Fe • Suzanne Ortiz – *house manager* • Dolores Zigil – *liason planning* • Lisa Samuels • Cielo

SEDUCTIVE ENTERTAINING

Britta Bollinger – *floral design* • Ashley Cate – *invitations and calligraphy;* EVENING IN RED: A.K. Vogel Photography • All Occasions Party Rentals, Knoxville, TN

FASHION

Book Cover: Reem Acra – *dress* • page 6: Prada – *dress, jacket* • page 8: Prada – *dress* • page 16: Yves Saint Laurent – *dress* • page 34: Bill Blass – *dress* • Christian Louboutin – *shoes* • pages 36–37: Donna Karan – *purse* • Christian Louboutin – *shoes* • La Perla – *slip* • pages 36–37, 60–61, 96–97, 102–103: Frette – *bed linens* • page 43: Prada – *pajamas* • pages 48–49: Gucci – *handbag, jacket* • Prada – *shoes* • Stephen Webster – *cufflinks* • page 53: Gucci – *dress, belt* • page 98: Oscar de la Renta – *dress* • Marchesa – *crystal-embroidered clutch* • Judith Leiber – *crystal handbag* • pages 113–114, 128, 132–133, 140–142: Matteo – *bed linens* • page 146: Donna Karan – *dress* • page 149: Donna Karan – *dress* • Christian Louboutin – *shoes* • page 150: Donna Karan – *dress* • page 160: Prada – *dress, shoes* • page 172: Naeem Khan – *dress* • page 157: Oscar de la Renta – *dress*

ART

Pages 22–23: David Braly • pages 36–37: Patrick Gordon, Fischbach Gallery – *paintings* • page 39: Kimber Berry, Bill Lowe Gallery • page 43: David Braly – *ceiling* • page 48: Lael Weyenberg, McLarry Fine Art Gallery • page 65: Anton Weiss, Bennett Galleries • page 71: Jeff Faust, Meyer East Gallery • page 72: Richard Currier, Lowe Gallery • page 86: Ronald Baldwin • page 95: Denis Perrollaz • page 97: Allen Cox, Bennett Galleries • page 103: Amanda Norman • page 108: Ray Turner, Meyer East Gallery • page 110: Braldt Bralds, Meyer East Gallery • pages 114–115: Poteet Victory, McLarry Modern • page 119: Bennett Galleries – *paintings* • page 129: Chris Richter, www.chrisrichterart.com • page 135: Bennett Galleries – *paintings* • page 137: Anton Weiss, Bennett Galleries • page 141: Robin Surber, Bennett Galleries

223

Published by Moll Anderson Productions
265 Brookview Town Centre Way, Suite 501, Knoxville, Tennessee 37919

Printed in United States of America
10 9 8 7 6 5 4 3 2 1

EAN: 978-1-937268-01-5

All Interior Design: Moll Anderson, Moll Anderson Productions

Cover & Interior Book Design: Sheri Ferguson, Ferguson Design Studio,
    and Moll Anderson, Moll Anderson Productions

Photo Styling: Moll Anderson, Moll Anderson Productions

Pre-production Design: Ashley Cate, Moll Anderson Productions

Managing Editor: Cindy Games, Moll Anderson Productions

Copyeditor: Billie Brownell, Cover to Cover Editorial Services

Floral Designer: Britta Bollinger in conjunction with Moll Anderson Productions

Cover Photography: Michael Gomez, Gomez Photography

Hair & Makeup: Brady Wardlaw

www.mollanderson.com

Eric Adkins: 82, 92–95, 98

beall + thomas: 14–15, 18–30, 31 (lower right and left), 32–33, 36–37, 39, 40–41, 44–50, 52–53, 55–67, 69, 71–72, 73 (upper and lower right), 74–77, 152 (lower), 158, 160–163, 168–175, 177–179

Michael Gomez: 6, 8, 10, 12–13, 16–17, 31 (upper right and left), 34, 43, 73 (lower left), 78–80, 84–91, 96–97, 100–103, 154, 156–157, 164–167, 176

John Hall: 104–143

A.K. Vogel Photography: 144, 146–147, 149, 150, 152 (upper and middle), 153